you are what you shite

you are what you shite

Dr Julian Keech

First published in Great Britain in 2005 by
Michael O'Mara Books Limited
9 Lion Yard
Tremadoc Road
London SW4 7NQ

A CIP catalogue record for this book is available from the British Library

ISBN - 1-84317-166-X

www.mombooks.com

Designed and typeset by Design 23

Printed and bound in Germany by GGP Media GmbH, Pößneck

CONTENTS

INTRODUCTION

Many of us can look back on apparently trivial incidents that changed our lives for ever. For Isaac Newton, it was the apple falling on his head; for Vlad the Impaler, it was seeing that first kebab; for our next-door neighbour, it was failing to spot the steamroller in time; for me, it was falling in a cowpat at the age of three. I refused to let my mother wash it off for a month and even when the novelty of always getting a train compartment to ourselves had worn off, I remained eager to find out more about the messy goo with the consistency – and indeed the taste – of Granny Bateman's gravy. My fascination with faeces continued at school. While other boys collected football stickers or stamps, I preferred to scour the playing field for the droppings of rabbits, hedgehogs, or, if I was really lucky, Kevin Warner from 4C. To me, happiness was a warm turd. I was the only boy at school who actually enjoyed having his head put down the toilet.

After university, I ran my own business, Jools' Stools, selling novelty items, including chocolate logs, plastic poops and our best-selling line, a commemorative turd in the shape of

Queen Juliana of the Netherlands. Unfortunately, the business folded just as we were about to introduce excrement figures of Brotherhood of Man to mark the tenth anniversary of their unforgettable *Eurovision Song Contest* triumph. Undeterred, I have since been fortunate enough to realize my dream of becoming a professional scatologist.

The wonderful thing about studying shite is that your work is never done. It really is a big job. For, just when you think you've seen every possible shape, colour and form of turd, someone produces a new strain. It's a bit like growing roses, but with less of a market for pot-pourri. Although no longer in that first flush of youth, I never tire of taking a dump. It is the most rewarding and fulfilling experience I know. Sometimes just for the hell of it, I overdose on prunes so that I can go four or five times a day. Sheer ecstasy! A friend of mine chooses the opposite course and opts for constipation. Last year he read the *Lord of the Rings* trilogy in one sitting. And shite runs in our family. There must be skid marks in our genes. My brother has a collection of over seventy ties with interesting poo motifs and my sister got married in a brown wedding dress, although that was partly to hide her nerves.

My passion for poop remains undiminished despite the fact that my wife has insisted that I no longer bring my work home – at least not in my lunchbox. My mission in life is to spread the word of muck to others. So next time you sit down on a warm toilet seat, think of those who have passed before you. Remember, each time you open your bowels you are also opening a world of enchantment, a packet of golden wonder. For, like snowflakes, no two shites are ever the same.

I am greatly indebted to Rod Green at Michael O'Mara for allowing me to talk shite. And if you want to meet like-minded souls, you can always log on to www.poopreport.com to exercise your brown matter. Happy crapping.

Dr Julian Keech.

After a pleasant scratching comes an unpleasant smarting.

DANISH PROVERB

a brief history
of shite

(in chronological ordure)

A long time ago BC: Adam went for a dump behind a bush in the Garden of Eden. Eve mistook it for a snake.

2500 BC: The first sitting-style toilets were introduced in Egypt, but most people still dug a hole in the ground.

200 BC: Wealthy Romans used private toilets. The Romans were so intrigued by faeces that they had their own god of dung, Stercutius.

1016: Edmund Ironside, King of Southern England, was emptying his bowels on the long wooden lavatory box in his home, unaware that one of his knights, Edric Streona, was lurking in the pit below. As Edmund sat down, Streona thrust his sword up the king's anal passage, killing him instantly.

1183: Holy Roman Emperor, Frederick I, lost some of his most trusted allies in central Europe following a messy tragedy at Erfurt castle. Summoned to the great hall for an important meeting, eight princes and several knights plunged to their deaths when the wooden floor gave way and sent them tumbling into the castle cesspool, where they drowned in a sea of excrement.

'They fell into where?
Now we're all in the shit . . .'

1355: Edward III looked into the piles of human dung that were forming in London's streets and rivers after being dumped there by passers-by.

1391: China produced the first toilet paper, each sheet measuring 2ft by 3ft (0.6m by 0.9m). It was available for emperors only.

1450: The close-stool became the preferred toilet for the upper classes. It consisted of a chamber pot inside a wooden box, thereby enabling the user to sit instead of squat while defecating.

1500: Joanna of Castile gave birth to Charles V, the future Holy Roman Emperor, while sitting on a Ghent lavatory.

1596: Sir John Harington invented the first flushing toilet, the Ajax water closet, priced 6s 8d (34p), and presented it to his godmother, Queen Elizabeth I. He recommended flushing it once a day, but she was so horrified that she refused to try it and banished him from court. For the next two hundred years those who weren't part of the effluent society continued to use the earth toilet or a basic pot or to drop their load in the local river. For those granted the comparative luxury of a pot, the practice was simply to throw the contents out of the nearest window after defecation. Afternoon walkers could then experience the smell of the country even in the heart of the town.

1760: Death on the throne. King George II was an enthusiastic and highly accomplished farter, but one evening he overdid it while sitting on the toilet, attempting to rid himself of constipation. A valet heard a noise described as 'louder than the usual royal wind' and found George lying dead on the floor. He had fallen off the toilet and banged his head on a cabinet.

1827: Beethoven's last movement.

1857: New Yorker Joseph C. Gayetty produced the first packaged toilet paper, called 'The Therapeutic Paper'. It was sold in packs of 500 for 50 cents with Gayetty's name printed on each sheet.

1884: Thomas Crapper perfected the flushing toilet.

1890: The Scott Paper Company of Philadelphia manufactured the first toilet tissue on a roll. Its catchy advertising said that 'over 65 per cent of middle-aged men and women suffer from some form of rectal disease,' and that 'harsh toilet tissue may cause serious injury.'

'Harsh toilet paper never caused me any harm!'
'Yes, and you're a total arsehole.'

1917: While stationed in Britain during the First World War, American soldiers noticed the name of Thomas Crapper & Company on London toilets and began announcing that they were 'going to the Crapper.' When this was then shortened to 'crap', a new word entered the lavatorial language.

1969: US astronaut Buzz Aldrin became the first man to have a shite on the moon when he used the 'fecal containment bag' attached to his spacesuit. Because of the zero gravity, the poo in the fecal bags often escaped while the astronauts were trying to dispose of it. Mission control tried to keep the need for defecation to a minimum by restricting the amount of fibre in the astronauts' diets.

1977: The passing of Elvis Presley. Elvis's drug habit was so bad that he had to take pills to regulate his bowel movements. On 16 August, he tried to relieve days of constipation in the bathroom at his Graceland mansion, but the strain proved too much for his bloated body and he suffered a fatal heart attack. He was found lying on the bathroom floor, his pyjama pants around his ankles. At least he didn't crap on his blue suede shoes.

1980: Archaeologists in York discovered a thousand-year-old Viking turd beneath a branch of Lloyds Bank. The Lloyds Bank Turd, as it became known in defecation circles, was an exciting find because it was in almost mint condition, making it highly collectable. It has since been insured for over £20,000. It is well worth spending a penny to see it at the city's Jorvik Viking Centre.

2005: Paula Radcliffe squatted by the roadside during the London Marathon complaining of 'stomach cramps'. Was she going for gold?

You know whatta you do when you shit? Singing, it's the same thing, only up!

ENRICO CARUSO

going through
the motions

The joy of excrement is not to be sniffed at. It is one of the seven wonders of the human body, along with navel fluff, ear wax, nostril hair, verrucae, whiteheads, and big crusty bogeys. But, when I appear on television chat shows or hang around the public lavatories on Hampstead Heath, I am amazed by how little people seem to know about the precise mechanics of defecation. The human digestive system is an intricate network of piping that would warrant any plumber charging double time. Think of an anaconda squashed into a matchbox and you'll get the general idea. Food takes between fifteen and thirty hours to pass through the entire system. From the mouth, it descends to the stomach where it is broken down by continual churning and also by the action of hydrochloric acid and digestive enzymes secreted by the stomach lining. When the food has been converted to a semi-liquid consistency, it passes into the duodenum where it is broken down still further by bile salts and acids released from the liver. The pancreas also releases digestive juices into the duodenum, and these juices contain enzymes that break down carbohydrates, fats, and proteins. The final breakdown occurs in the small intestine. While beneficial nutrients are absorbed through the intestinal lining into either the bloodstream or the lymphatic system, the food residue passes into the large intestine where much of the water it contains is absorbed by the lining of the colon. It is in the large intestine that the turd solidifies and, because of the water absorption, the longer it remains in the intestine, the drier the end product will be.

'Don't worry, Miss Clench. I'd say you've got one coming through about Wednesday.'

Finally the undigested waste matter is expelled, via the rectum and anus, as faeces. Of the pounds of food you eat each day, only about a third comes out as poo.

So what's in a turd? Well, faeces consist of indigestible food residue, dead bacteria (which may account for as much as half the weight of the turd), dead cells shed from the intestinal lining, secretions from the intestine (such as mucus), bile from the liver, and water. About three-quarters of the average turd is water, although, not surprisingly, the content for diarrhoea is considerably higher. It is the bile that gives your poop that lovely warm brown colour. The main pigment found in bile is called bilirubin, which is produced by the breakdown of haemoglobin, the pigment in red blood cells. Just as the iron in haemoglobin gives blood its red colour, so the iron in bilirubin makes turds brown. As for the distinctive smell, that is a result of the bacterial action. Bacteria produce compounds such as indole, skatole, and mercaptans, which are rich in sulphur, as well as the inorganic gas, hydrogen sulphide, the original 'bad eggs gas'. These are the same compounds responsible for the smell of a really impressive fart. Truly, the world would be a poorer place without hydrogen sulphide.

Ninety per cent of people in western countries have a bowel pattern that ranges from three bowel movements a day to four a week. The latter works out at one per episode of

EastEnders, thereby establishing another link between shite and *EastEnders*. But it is possible to move your bowels every day and still be constipated if the stools are hard and difficult to pass. Equally, a daily bowel movement is by no means essential, nor is it necessarily indicative of good health. So the only hard and fast rule is that if it's hard and fast, you're not constipated.

Not without reason has it been said that constipation is the thief of time. My fellow experts have calculated that a quarter of the world's population suffers from constipation at some time in their lives, mainly in the west, where our diet often lacks sufficient fibre. Fibre, which is found in foods such as wholemeal bread, fresh fruit and vegetables, provides the bulk that the muscles of the colon (the major part of the large intestine) need to stimulate propulsion of the faeces and is, therefore, directly linked to constipation. A lack of fibre in your diet saves on only one thing – toilet paper.

You can tell a lot about a person from the colour of their stools. In many ways a stool is like a star sign. Russell Grant probably does his own daily column. So here is your easy-to-keep lavatorial colour chart:

Black: A black, tarry poop can be an indication of bleeding in the stomach, duodenum, or small intestine. It may be a novelty, but go and see a doctor.

Conker brown: Hard and dark is a sure sign of constipation, which probably means you're eating too much white bread, cake and sugar and not enough fresh fruit and vegetables. A daily dose of prunes should do the trick, while still retaining the colour. Soft and dark is often the result of unusually large amounts of iron or red wine in the diet. There is nothing wrong with this, but removing the marks from the bowl does tend to use up extra Domestos, so switch to Sauvignon Blanc for a while.

Brown streaked with red: The red veins are blood and are caused by a variety of ailments. Haemorrhoids are the most common cause of rectal bleeding, resulting in small amounts of bright red blood being found on the surface of the faeces or on toilet paper. An anal fissure, often originating from a tear in the lining of the anus caused by the passage of hard, dry faeces, can also produce a bloody stool. Here too, the amount of blood in evidence should be small. If there is enough for a transfusion, it could be something more serious.

'I'm telling you it was striped like a tiger's tail!'

Dark red: If the entire stool takes on a dark red hue, this may be a sign of a colon disorder. Alternatively, it could be caused by a beetroot fixation. So unless you're Polish, get it checked out by a doctor.

Hazelnut brown: Congratulations! You have a relatively healthy diet.

Yellow: Pale faeces may be due to a blockage of the bile duct or to malabsorption caused by a high fat content. Fatty faeces are invariably oily, frothy, highly pungent, and difficult to flush away. You'll know when you've dropped one . . . and so will everybody else. Another cause of yellow stools is an inherited condition called Gilbert's disease, which affects around 2 per cent of the population. Although it is most common among teenage boys, there is actually no known link to loud music, pornographic magazines and masturbation – instead it is caused by a deficiency in the liver where red blood cells are broken down. People with Gilbert's disease don't process as many blood cells and so their stools tend to be yellow from the lower amount of discarded red blood cell matter. It may look disturbing but it's perfectly harmless. However, if your stools are yellow and runny, it's a different story.

Diarrhoea and constipation are the terrible twins of defecation, the Bros of the bowels. The most obvious symptom of diarrhoea is a faster evacuation than Dunkirk, but when a hard, constipated plug blocks the passage, it creates a situation whereby only the liquid stool from higher up in the bowel can be passed. This is known as bypass diarrhoea, and not simply because it often happens on the M25. Diarrhoea is like vomiting except that instead of food coming back up from your stomach, it is digested food, already in the intestines, that is in a hurry to get through your system. Diarrhoea is caused by irritation in the intestines, resulting in the bowel passing its contents too fast for the water to be absorbed by the intestine walls. The food mush keeps getting wetter and wetter as the intestine muscles push it out quickly and instead of dry poop, you get the runs. Several things can cause the intestinal irritation: unfamiliar foods, food poisoning, food intolerance, a virus, or anxiety. And if you weren't anxious beforehand, you certainly will be once you realize you've got diarrhoea.

Scientists investigating the ailment have found that certain words can also bring on an attack of diarrhoea. These include:

'Quick, hide, my husband's home!'

'Didn't you notice there was a hole in the condom?'

'Don't you think it's time we got married?'

'Mummy's coming to stay for three weeks.'

'I'm from the Inland Revenue.'

'I thought you knew I had gonorrhoea.'

'It's triplets!'

Orange: When it comes to stools, babies can manage a veritable rainbow of colours. As well as green and blue offerings, when they take in milk their poos turn yellow (pale yellow with bottlefed, golden yellow to a mustard shade with breastfed), and finally, when they progress to solids, it is a case of what goes in must come out. If you feed a four-month-old baby puréed carrot, the contents of the next nappy will be bright orange. This is particularly useful if trying to locate it in the middle of the night.

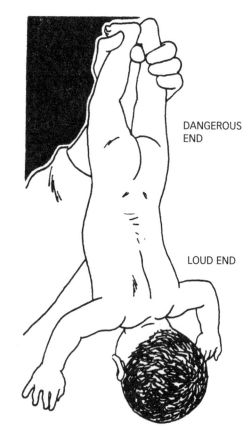

DANGEROUS END

LOUD END

Green: Adults can produce a green poop if they eat a diet rich in leafy, green vegetables. But be warned: this can create an effect similar to the condition popularly known as 'vegetarians' fart'. Babies' stools may be green if they are taking in too much lactose (the natural sugar found in milk), or when they are introduced to food for the first time.

Blue: Rather like the blue rose, the blue turd remains elusive in adults, although it is hoped that future research into dietary needs may one day produce an azure beauty. The answer may lie with children's faeces since babies *are* capable of dropping a blue poop, either as a result of illness or through consuming large quantities of food colouring, notably in ice cream.

White: You can do white poop after consuming a barium milkshake in order to have an X-ray of the upper gastrointestinal tract.

Those who aim at great deeds must also suffer greatly.

PLUTARCH

bathroom habits

As revealing as their poos are a person's bathroom habits. How you sit, how you wipe, how you behave: all of these offer major clues regarding your character. Check your potty personality:

King John: This guy likes to take his time in the bathroom and enjoys prolonging the experience by incorporating reading matter or crossword puzzles. His family know that this is his quality time and that he must never be disturbed.

DR JULIAN'S ANALYSIS: He has probably spent his life juggling career and a family, with the result that the toilet is his only place of refuge. And whereas his wife smells his breath when he comes home from the pub, she is unlikely to carry out a similar test to determine whether he's actually had a crap while in the bathroom. Likely occupation: Company middle management. Lucky colour: Brown.

The Shameless Shitter: This person makes as much noise as possible in the act of defecation and doesn't care who hears it. A rutting wildebeest would be quieter. He or she is likely to pass a loud exclamation at the moment of release, followed up by calls, text messages or even photos from their mobile phone. In a public toilet, they will merrily conduct a conversation with a friend in the next cubicle.

DR JULIAN'S ANALYSIS: This person is a born exhibitionist, a gregarious partygoer who has to be the centre of attention. Hell is a Findus dinner for one. Likely occupation: Secretary/factory worker. Lucky colour: Brown.

'Here's a photo of one of my best efforts.'

Mr Time and Motion: There is no fuss about this busy chap. He's in and out like a dose of Ex-lax. The paper is used sparingly but efficiently; he doesn't exert more effort than is absolutely necessary and he never forgets to put the seat down afterwards or to wash his hands. The whole performance is conducted with military precision.

DR JULIAN'S ANALYSIS: Here is a man in command of his own destiny. Supremely confident, he makes Jose Mourinho look like Syd Little. He has no time to waste on trivialities such as going to the toilet. Single-minded and determined, he is a money-making machine who is either divorced or has a mistress at weekends. Likely occupation: Bank manager or lawyer. Lucky colour: Brown.

The Compulsive Cleaner: This person cannot resist the temptation to tidy up in the bathroom . . . even while you're sitting on the toilet. She – and it is invariably a woman who falls into this category – will pick up any stray scraps of toilet paper from around your ankles and immaculately rearrange the roll just as you're really concentrating hard. And barely has the first trickle of flush washed down the sides of the bowl than she is in there making sure there are no unsightly stains.

DR JULIAN'S ANALYSIS: This person is impatient and so fanatically tidy that she could well be a member of the Kim and Aggie Liberation Front. She is most likely a mother whose children have grown up and left home, and for whom a bottle of bleach has become a child substitute. Likely occupation: Waiter in a Chinese restaurant. Lucky colour: Brown.

Captain Chaos: You know immediately when this person has been using the toilet. The seat is up, there are skid marks around the bowl, and the toilet roll is trailing along the wet floor. And their motto is: if at first your turd doesn't flush away, give up. Nor would they ever dream of replacing a toilet roll. Instead, the next user reaches out to find nothing but a roll of cardboard.

DR JULIAN'S ANALYSIS: This is someone who is selfish, unreliable, almost certainly male, and probably has difficulty sustaining a relationship. Likely occupation: Builder. Lucky colour: Brown.

Buffalo Bill: This guy is no shrinking violet. Instead of sitting quietly on the toilet, he rides it for all he is worth, rocking the seat back and forth, forcing the turd to come out quicker than it really wants to. This performance is usually accompanied by wholesale grunting.

DR JULIAN'S ANALYSIS: This is someone who relishes a challenge, who doesn't want to live life in the bus lane. By taking on the chestnut demon at its own game, he is tackling a foe that, as he well knows, can cause him considerable grief if things go wrong. He is like a matador with a bull. But that's what gives him his kicks. Likely occupation: Stockbroker. Lucky colour: Brown.

The Hoverer: This individual hovers outside the bathroom door while you're taking a dump and asks how long you're going to be, seemingly unaware that the interruption merely delays the entire evacuation process. Even when you think they've gone, you can still see their shadow lurking beneath the door.

DR JULIAN'S ANALYSIS: For some adults a trip to the toilet is like a child's visit to the sweetshop. If your friend goes for a crap, you immediately want one, too. And if there's only one loo in the house, this can lead to hovering. It is a nasty, unsavoury habit, born out of envy, and a persistent hoverer can make an irritable bowel positively homicidal. Likely occupation: Sales assistant. Lucky colour: Brown.

The Paranoid Pooper: This person is acutely embarrassed about ever having to go to the toilet and keeps visits as discreet and infrequent as possible. MI5's movements are less secretive. He or she will even place a thick wad of toilet paper in the bottom of the bowl beforehand to deaden the sound of the drop. Ironically, this often has the effect of attracting unwanted attention since the toilet clogs up and overflows. Terrified of being caught with their pants down, they are particularly averse to using public conveniences where they imagine every piece of flaky paint is concealing a spy-hole.

DR JULIAN'S ANALYSIS: This individual has probably been through some traumatic lavatorial experience in the past – perhaps a ducking at school, an embarrassing overflow, or a parent running off with a toilet attendant. The phobia is most common among single women of a certain age and extends to using half a roll of toilet paper to wipe off the smallest mark, just to be sure. Prefers *Songs of Praise* to Gordon Ramsay and thinks fast food is the tool of the devil. Likely occupation: Personal assistant. Unlucky colour: Brown.

'I'm sure someone must have heard that plop.'

poop scoops

In Bali, Indonesia, small dogs act as mobile nappie-wipes by licking clean a baby's poo immediately following defecation. So, when a Balinese mother carries her baby, the family dog accompanies her.

Each day, on average, people produce one ounce (28.35 g) of poo for every 12 pounds (5.4 kg) of their body weight.

Grieving aboriginal widows used to wear human excrement on their heads as a mark of mourning.

Allowing for babies, children, and people in poorer countries whose poops weigh less because they eat less, the average turd weighs about eight ounces (226.8 g). With a world population of 6.521 billion, this means that the planet produces around 3,260,500,000 pounds (1,482,045,400 kg) of shite per day.

Pooper scoopers date back to Victorian England when small boys would collect dog dirt from city streets and sell it to tanners for use in tanning leather.

According to legend, mistletoe originated from a bird that left its faeces on a tree branch. In German, the word *mist* means dung and in some European cultures mistletoe represents dung as well as love and fertility.

In some of the poorer parts of the world, people use 'flying toilets' – they crap in a plastic bag and then throw it as far away as possible. A woman in a Nairobi ghetto recently complained about the piles of excrement on the roof of her shack.

To fall a log at last,
dry, bald and sere:
A lily of a day

BEN JONSON

the pants-hiker's guide to the lavatory

I find it sad, nay, distressing, that even in these supposedly enlightened days of the twenty-first century some people say to me at dinner parties: 'But Julian, surely a turd is just a turd.' Not so. For just as there are different varieties of cheese or different types of lawyer, so there are many different forms of turd. I myself have identified no fewer than forty-five species of faeces, many procured on expeditions to the Turd World. Only last year while on holiday in Peru, I thought I had uncovered a rare gem in a remote bog near the foothills of the Andes. It was brown and flaky and like no other I had seen before. Alas, my joy was cut short by the discarded Cadbury's wrapper. My greatest ambition is that one day I will have a piece of excrement named after me – something to hand down to my grandchildren. In the meantime, my fellow scatologists continue to scour the globe for new forms of floater, Klingon and python, hoping perhaps to stumble across a specimen of the elusive Iranian King Bullet, or to give it its Latin name, *tehranasorearse rex*. Consequently, the list below is by no means exhaustive, although it would be if you did them one after another.

The Sultana: Experts consider this to be the most frustrating of all poops. You spend half an hour on the toilet, straining and sweating as if about to give birth, but all you have to show for it at the end is a small plop resembling a sultana.

The Floater: One of the most familiar types, characterized by its remarkable ability to float in the bowl, often in small bitesize chunks.

The Oliver Twist Floater: A sub-species of the common floater, this persistent little fellow continually resurfaces despite repeated flushings. In extreme cases, it can take an entire Bank Holiday Monday to get rid of one. It gets its name because it keeps coming back for more.

The Phantom: This mysteriously appears in the toilet and no one will admit to putting it there. Most commonly found in areas with a high student population.

The Hanger: A poo that simply refuses to let go, hence its alternative name of 'The Jewish Mother'. Just as you are about to release, it hangs there in limbo, seemingly suspended between your anus and the water. Sometimes a rocking or bouncing motion will eventually achieve the desired effect, but there are occasions when the only solution is to knock it off with a piece of toilet paper or any other convenient implement. However, a toothbrush is not recommended.

The Ghost: You feel it come out and you know you've done it, but when you wipe there is nothing on the paper and there is no sign of any poo in the toilet. Spooky or what?

The Second Thought: Just when you think you have finished and have painstakingly wiped yourself clean and pulled your pants back on, you realise to your horror that there is more to come.

'Oh, no! There's more to come!'

The Pebbledash: Among the most feared of all bowel movements. In a desperate race against time to get to the toilet, it is a question of whether the bottom falls out of your world before the world falls out of your bottom. No sooner do you sit down than thousands of golden granules shoot out faster than the speed of light and splatter all over the sides of the bowl, under the rim and over your bare cheeks. Rather like sperm in search of the egg, one or two may even achieve the Holy Grail for diarrhoea – by reaching the ceiling. The act of wiping may use up most of your annual holiday leave.

The Lesser Pebbledash: A more restrained version of the Common Pebbledash, this confines itself to splattering over the lower half of the bowl. It is usually the result of six pints of lager and a Mexican, as opposed to eight pints and a Vindaloo.

The Splashback: A nice clean exit like an Olympic diver, but the point of entry into the water is slightly askew, so that it splashes back and soaks your cheeks. Highly prized in certain districts of France for combining the toilet and bidet in one.

The Python: Also known as 'The Monster', 'King Kong' or 'The Anaconda'. This most terrifying of turds is, nonetheless, immensely satisfying. Usually painless and of excellent soft texture, it emerges unbroken, and it is not until you turn around and look into the bowl that you realise just what you have achieved. For there it stands, proud and erect, head rearing out of the water, daring you to try and flush it away. You have no idea how long it is – although it is inevitably embellished to several feet when the tale is recounted to fellow enthusiasts – because the end disappears into the U-bend rather like a train going into a tunnel on the Victoria Line. While the act of emission is straightforward, that of disposal is considerably more problematic. Ancient remedies include several bowls of water, a wire coathanger, or a large howitzer but, in the absence of a police frogman, sometimes there is no alternative but to take the matter into your own hands and break it in two. The rats in the sewers check their life insurance policies when they know one of these is on the way.

The Surprise Package: A shite that comes along unexpectedly, without warning, at the most inappropriate time – for example, during your wedding, during sex, or while undergoing root canal surgery.

The Sentry: This tiny, round, hard nugget appears so insignificant that you wonder whether it was actually worth going to the toilet. It is only when you finally squeeze him out that you realise he was holding back two gallons of scorching, smelly, brown, frothy liquid.

The Strangeways: Shard-like pieces of crap tear your rectum, causing you to bleed and making you feel as if you've been gang-raped by sex-starved prisoners.

The Groaner: A log so mighty and seemingly immovable that it cannot exit without vocal accompaniment.

The Cowpat: A motion, erring on the soft side, that lacks downward propulsion. Instead of landing in the water, it makes an ominous splat and spreads out laterally, covering both cheeks like a layer of brown instant whip. By the time you've wiped it clean, the Andrex puppy has had puppies of her own.

The Trumpet: As a result of a build-up of gas and usually a delay in reaching the toilet, this one is immediately preceded by a blast of sound reminiscent of Kenny Ball and his Jazzmen. The noise also serves as a warning for others to steer clear of the bathroom for at least the next hour.

'For God's sake steer clear of the bathroom!'

The Snake Charmer: A long, slender poo which has managed to coil itself into a threatening, but ultimately harmless, position. According to an insider, this was the type of turd chosen for the defecation scene in the movie *Austin Powers: International Man of Mystery*.

The Duracel Bunny: This one just keeps going . . . and going . . . and going.

The Sweetcorn: A firm stool, dotted with generous helpings of yellow sweetcorn. Its unique topping makes this a much sought-after specimen and invariably comes as a surprise to the deliverer, particularly if he or she can't remember having eaten any sweetcorn.

The FIFA: A beautifully crafted, round turd, consisting of a dozen or more small, dark pellets intricately woven together to give the overall appearance of the panels of a football. It is always welcome since it invariably follows a lengthy bout of constipation.

The Scorcher: Fiery, golden and loose, this is the Sally Webster of *excreta*. The burning 'aftertaste' parts your cheeks like the Red Sea and renders the simple act of sitting down well nigh impossible for at least fifteen minutes.

The Side Birth: This one hurts so much that you would swear (and swearing is not uncommon during this delivery) that it must be coming out sideways.

The Colgate: Soft and rarely satisfactory, this comes out like toothpaste and seems to continue for an inordinately long time, running the risk of piling up to your cheeks while you sit there helpless.

The Titanic: A huge log glides down the slipway, then breaks in two before sinking.

The Toxic: The ultimate killing machine. Produces a scent that lingers long into the night and, because of its capacity to destroy any romantic intentions, is the most effective form of contraception known to man. It has been held responsible for wrecking many a relationship, hence the expression 'to dump your girlfriend'.

The Jack-in-the Box: You flush. It disappears. Then suddenly it pops back out again.

The Marble Effect: First discovered in Lavatorial Guinea, this perennial favourite takes the form of a succession of cute rabbit droppings that make tiny splashing sounds as they hit the water. Top of the plops with many enthusiasts.

The Bastard: A beast of a log, hard and unyielding, that simply refuses to venture beyond the release point in your rectum. It will even get as far as peeking out into daylight but, like a child who is afraid of the water, is unwilling to make the final splash. Instead it sits there, blocking the entrance to your passage for up to two hours, while you desperately try and force it to go that extra mile. Some try breaking off the end with a pair of Marigolds; others simply suck it back up, but neither remedy is effective and to date experts have been unable to find a cure for this most distressing of conditions. Ultimately, the only solution is to persist even though it feels as if you are about to pass a bowling ball. When it does eventually emerge it leaves a vacuous air space in the rectum for up to twenty-four hours and is therefore much prized in the gay community. Most specialists agree that this was the crap that killed Elvis on what was undoubtedly scatology's brownest day.

The Peek-a-Boo: A less dangerous version of 'The Bastard'. Now you see it, now you don't. This log is playing games with you. Requires patience and muscle control.

The Skidder: On the face of it, a perfectly ordinary, undetectable poo, until you look in the pan and see a series of skid marks worthy of Michael Schumacher on a wet day at Silverstone. This form is most common when visiting somebody else's house.

The Cannon: This one is halfway out when it is suddenly shot out like a cannonball as the result of an unexpectedly loud fart. The Cannon is most common when someone you are trying hard to impress – your boss, a potential major investor, your new girlfriend — is waiting outside the door.

The Boomerang: A long, soft log with a bend in the middle so that both ends protrude above the water. It derives its name from the fact that, because of its distinctive shape, it does not flush away easily and keeps coming back. A real collector's item.

'I nudge Klingons off
with my pipe . . .'

'. . . while I find a credit
card is just the thing!'

The Klingon: A seemingly troublefree business in which a
suitable pile nestles quietly in the water. However, the naïve and
inexperienced can be lulled into premature wiping, unaware of
the presence of a Klingon, which, when coming into contact with
paper, will smear horribly. Wise heads simply wait patiently for
the last Klingon to drop off, even if it means missing dinner.

The Teflon: The crème de la crème of human excrement. It slides out immaculately and when you come to wipe, there is not a mark on the paper. Totally satisfying, this is the multiple orgasm of defecation. It leaves a smile on your face for the rest of the day.

The Chinese: Half an hour after having one, you need to go again.

The Gripper: A sticky customer that manifests itself by adhering to the hairs around the back passage, thus making wiping a lengthy and painful experience. A King Gripper has been known to reduce a grown man to tears. Grippers usually occur when the phone is ringing in another room.

The Emergency Plumber: A flat poop of such majestic proportions that it plugs up the toilet, causing it to overflow. The only winner is the plumber who collects his call-out fee.

The Wish: You sit there and fart a couple of times but nothing solid comes out.

The Bomb: The shape and colour of a Christmas pudding, this explodes from your backside with a vengeance, leaving a dark telltale mark on the base of the bowl. Unlike other varieties, it remains intact, although cases have been reported of three or more Bombs being dropped in one raid. So firm that it could be used as a house-building material, the Bomb is often the result of a change in medication.

The Gas Chamber: Only ever found in public conveniences, this greenish concoction has been sitting in a clogged-up bowl beneath a pile of old toilet paper for several weeks. Consequently, as soon as the door opens, it emits the most noxious of fumes, forcing the would-be dumper to seek an alternative cubicle . . . quickly.

The Archer: Behaves perfectly until it hits the water line, at which point it shoots a single spurt of ice-cold fluid up and into your still-open back passage. A truly chilling experience.

The Limpet: This clever little chap sticks to the bowl below water level and cannot be flushed unless prized away by a stiff brush.

The Steamer: Walnut brown in colour and with a soft, creamy texture, this eagerly anticipated mound of dung emits enough steam to heat a small village.

The Crowd Pleaser: The kind of poo that is so intriguing in size and/or appearance that you have to show it to someone before flushing.

HOW DO WE WIPE?

A recent survey gave a fascinating insight into our wiping habits.

The average tear is 5.9 sheets of toilet paper.

44 per cent of users wipe from front to back from behind their backs.

60 per cent look at the paper after they wipe.

42 per cent fold the paper, 33 per cent crumple, 8 per cent both fold and crumple, and 6 per cent wrap it around their hands. The rest don't know.

50 per cent say they have wiped with leaves.

8 per cent have wiped with their hands.

2 per cent have wiped with money.

(source: www.home.nycap.rr.com)

poop scoops

A Canadian drunk driver with a taste for trickery tried to foil a police breathalyser machine in 2005 by stuffing his mouth full of faeces. After his Ford pickup truck was pulled over near Toronto, the fifty-nine-year-old man was taken to a nearby police station for testing, but on the way he vomited, urinated and defecated in the squad car. Then, at the station, he grabbed a handful of his own excrement and put it in his mouth in an attempt to fool the breathalyser. Alas, his cunning plan failed as the machine registered two readings of more than twice the legal blood alcohol limit. The arresting officer remarked: 'We get a lot of people in here talking shit but I've never heard of anything like this before. I don't think alcohol alone would make you do something as disgusting as that.'

A Chilean family narrowly escaped being crushed to death in 2002, when the tin roof of their home collapsed under the accumulated weight of fifteen years of pigeon droppings.

A KLM airliner had to return to Holland without its passengers after the floor of the cabin became filled with human excrement. The incident happened when the contents of two toilets were blown into the passengers' seating area. The toilet had a vacuum system to suck the excrement into a container but while the container was being emptied, the waste was blown back into the main cabin. Over 160 of the 282 passengers were affected. A KLM spokesman said ruefully: 'We won't be able to use the plane for a while.'

A ruthless gunman snatched a San Diego woman's bag in 2005, only to find that it contained nothing but poo from her dog Misty.

The body of an eighty-six-year-old Danish man was found sitting on the toilet of his home a year after he died. Police forced their way into the pensioner's home in Helsingor after neighbours reported a bad smell. Officers found a dated bottle of medicine next to the body, which proved that the victim had died at least a year previously while answering a call of nature. Neighbours described him as a loner.

poop scoops

Police in Bayreuth, Germany, are hunting pranksters who have been sticking miniature US flags into piles of dog poo in public parks. Since 2004 over three thousand piles of canine excrement have been claimed in what was originally thought to be a protest against the American-led invasion of Iraq. Police spokesman Reiner Kuechler said: 'We have sent out extra patrols to catch whoever is doing this in the act. But frankly, we don't know what we would do if we caught them red-handed.' Legal experts say there is no law against using faeces as a flag stand and the federal constitution is vague on the subject.

In 2002 it was reported that a range of Melbourne dung mountains were giving Australian authorities a headache. The piles of dried excrement weighed nearly two million tonnes and were growing by about eighty thousand tonnes a year across Victoria. In some areas the heaps date back fifty years. While other states stored the waste for future use as compost or fuel, Victoria had yet to decide what to do with it all.

US chat show host Johnny Carson sparked a nationwide toilet paper shortage in 1973 after joking on *The Tonight Show* that the essential commodity was, like oil at the time, running low. Panic buyers, terrified of being caught short, rushed straight to supermarkets to grab all remaining stocks, the resultant empty shelves merely convincing consumers that the shortage was genuine. By noon on the day after the programme, most stores in America had sold out of toilet roll. Shops even tried to ration it but they couldn't keep up with demand. Manufacturers tried to soothe fears by showing their plants in full production, but even after Carson apologised on air, it was another three weeks before the scare died down.

This little steamer, like all her brave and battered sisters, is immortal.

J. B. PRIESTLEY

klingons on the starboard bow

The evolution of Man is a truly fascinating subject and Darwin didn't do a bad job considering it was pretty much his first book. However, one topic that he overlooked is that most intriguing of all human riddles: what did we wipe our bottoms with before the invention of toilet paper? I know it's difficult to imagine life Before Charmin (or BC as historians refer to it) but just as there was a time when there were no automobiles, no washing machines, no computers, and no Pot Noodle, so Man had to invent his own way of removing those unmentionable stains. His first answer to the problem of cleaning up his own excrement was to use the tools that God had put on this earth for him. But when Woman refused on the grounds that it would ruin her nails, he had to search elsewhere. As he foraged through the woods for hours on end in search of food for his family and to avoid the Jehovah's Witnesses whom he had heard were knocking door-to-door, Man took advantage of Nature's provisions. He would first use a twig to remove any hangers-on, and then he would wipe himself clean with a few large leaves. Since most early settlements were built on the banks of streams or rivers, he would also be able to squat in the water and wash around his anus. Whether he did this before or after using the twigs and leaves would determine the quality of the village's drinking water for the next few days.

Less enlightened souls simply used lumps of earth or, if they lived by the seaside, mussel shells. Understandably, no one wanted to catch crabs.

Always at the cutting edge of progress, Ancient Rome operated a class system. All public toilets had a sponge soaked in a bucket of brine and attached to the end of a stick, but the wealthy preferred wool and rosewater for that softer sensation. Discarded sheep's wool went on to become the material of choice for Viking England, although many of our continental cousins used a different currency of grass or straw. But the grass was often too rough and the straw too smooth and brittle, with the result that the implement tended to fall between two stools. Eskimos employed a combination of snow and tundra moss to achieve the desired effect; Spanish sailors used the frayed ends of old anchor cables; while on tropical islands such as Hawaii coconut shells were unsurprisingly deemed preferable to pineapples. Of course money talked, and members of the French royal family were able to wipe clean with lace. Elsewhere, eighteenth-century royalty used silk strips or soft goose feathers. While goose feathers ensured a gentle wipe, however, they were not stiff enough to perform the task thoroughly — a problem the royals overcame by leaving the feathers attached to the goose's neck, thereby obtaining the required leverage. It should be pointed out that the goose was too deceased to object.

In certain parts of India and the Arab world, the Western practice of using paper is to this day considered disgusting because people feel that it always leaves a residue. So instead they often use water or sand in combination with their left hand. Some historians believe this is why we shake hands with our right hands – because the left hand was traditionally the dirty hand. In the seventeenth century, a western traveller wrote how Muslim men wiped with stones or clods of earth, rinsed with water, and finally dried with linen cloth. Pious men were said to wear lumps of earth in their turbans and carry small pitchers of water solely for this purpose.

In colonial America they used corn cobs – in many respects an obvious choice given sweetcorn's apparent affinity with the human turd. But the invention of the printing press created fresh possibilities, and it quickly became clear that, both in terms of texture and content, daily newspapers were made for the (big) job. The British peerage opted for something weightier than bog standard newspapers. In the eighteenth century Lord

Chesterfield wrote in a letter to his son that one should always carry a cheap copy of the Latin poets to the toilet, not only for educational reading matter, but also to put each page to good use after reading it. Unfortunately, this led to the English landscape being littered with paper since there were no modern sewers to take it away.

In the late nineteenth century, the Sears catalogue became popular in rural America, and consumers were quick to spot its potential for wiping duties. People simply hung it up on a nail and enjoyed the free supply of hundreds of pages of absorbent, uncoated paper. However, the Sears catalogue fell from favour in the 1930s when it began being printed on glossy, clay-coated paper — a move that prompted hundreds of letters of complaint to the company in what literally amounted to a smear campaign.

poop scoops

The Aztec emperor Montezuma had a nephew, Cuitlahac, whose name meant 'plenty of excrement'.

Some Muslims will not sit on a toilet seat that has been occupied by other people. Instead, when confronted with a Western-style seat, they sometimes stand on it and squat in mid-air to avoid physical contact. Under such circumstances, accuracy is clearly of the essence.

Japanese psychiatrist Hiroyuki Nishigaki recommends constricting your anus one hundred times every day to relieve depression.

The average American uses fifty-seven sheets of toilet paper a day and over twenty thousand sheets a year. In the Pentagon alone, workers get through on average 666 rolls a day . . . the number of 'The Beast'.

Dog poo on the pavements leaves 650 Parisians hospitalized each year.

Given that we spend an average of six minutes a day defecating, if a man dies at eighty-five, he will have spent a total of 129 days (just over four months) of his life on the throne.

During the Gulf War the US military used toilet paper to camouflage their tanks in Saudi Arabia.

The germs present in human faeces can pass through up to ten layers of toilet paper.

In the United States dogs deposit 3.6 billion pounds (1.63 billion kg) of waste a year – that's enough to cover eight hundred football pitches in a layer of poop a foot (0.3 m) thick.

Never eat more than you can lift.

MISS PIGGY

the brown period

excrement as an art form

Thankfully, more and more people are beginning to see the artistic possibilities in human and animal excrement. How many of us have not looked back into the bowl at some time in our lives as we hitched up our pants and thought, 'That poo reminds me of Rodin's *The Thinker*', or 'I can see the faces of Ant and Dec in that turd'? Each time we defecate, we create an individual work of art. With so many creative talents beginning to see the light at the end of the passage, it can surely only be a matter of time before Wallace and Gromit are made from natural waste instead of expensive plasticine.

In 1961, avant-garde Italian artist Piero Manzoni produced ninety tins of *merda d'artista* (artist's shit). Each can contained 30 grams of his own faeces and Manzoni explained that his motivation was to expose the gullible nature of the art-buying public. The cans were sealed according to industrial standards and then circulated to different museums around the world. Manzoni himself died within two years of his groundbreaking creation, but his legacy lived on, and in 2002 London's Tate Gallery paid £22,300 for one of the cans, describing it as 'a seminal work.' Manzoni had originally sold his excrement as if it were gold, but the price paid by the Tate — £745 per gram –

actually exceeded the £550 per gram that the tin's contents would have cost had they been made of 24-carat gold. Shortly before his death, Manzoni told a friend: 'I hope these cans explode in the vitrines of the collectors.' This, too, has proved prophetic since at least half of the ninety cans have subsequently exploded.

French artist Chris Ofili won the prestigious 1998 Turner Prize, worth £20,000, by creating a painting from his favourite medium, elephant dung. He obtains regular supplies from London Zoo and dries them in an airing cupboard before use.

'Now when they say my paintings are crap at least I can agree.'

Italian artist Gilbert Proesch and his English partner George Passmore (known collectively as Gilbert and George) staged a show at the South London Art Gallery in 1995 entitled 'Naked Shit Pictures'. It consisted of sixteen large, glossy photos of themselves surrounded by a series of 'defecation motifs', including turd circles and turd sculptures. A more recent offering from the pair is 'The Flying Shit Wheel of Death', which features eight splattered bird droppings with a dead pigeon as its axle.

An art exhibition on the theme of excrement recently opened in Canada. 'Scatalogue: 30 Years of Crap in Contemporary Art' went on display at a gallery in Ottawa to demonstrate 'the last remaining taboo in contemporary art.' Exhibits included soiled trousers, freeze-fried dung, and a statue of former Canadian Prime Minister Brian Mulroney holding a turd in his hand. A local MP churlishly described the exhibition as a waste of taxpayers' money.

German artist Bernd Eilts turns dried cow poop into wall clocks and small sculptures. He is currently expanding into cow dung wristwatches. 'It helps to pass the time,' he explains.

Italian artist Monica Bonvicini recently unveiled a fully-functioning toilet as a public piece of art. The glass cube containing a usable loo was positioned opposite London's Tate Britain gallery. It was made from one-way glass, meaning that you could see out but not in.

An American firm called Turd Birds offers individually crafted models of birds made from genuine California horse excrement. Each turd is hand-selected by the artist for shape, consistency and colour with only the highest quality waste matter being used. It is then dried and sealed in liquid plastic to form the bird's body before twigs are added for the legs and beak. In recognition of the war in Iraq, the firm has introduced a new range of birds dressed as soldiers, known as Pooper Troopers. It claims: 'Pooper Troopers are the perfect companion for military families while their loved one is away.'

My beloved put his hand by the hole of the door and my bowels were moved for him.

SONG OF SOLOMON 4:1-7

motion
pictures

10 epic Hollywood dumps

The Hollywood moguls used to say that sex sold a movie, but, in everyday life, sex comes a very poor second to taking a dump. Consider the facts: if you go a week without sex, you feel the slight pain of frustration; if you go a week without taking a dump, you're in absolute agony. And if you've had a big hot curry the night before washed down with copious amounts of lager, which would you rather do first thing the next morning – fornicate or defecate? A good shite has so many advantages over sex. For example:

You don't have to offer words of reassurance or explanation after having a shite.

A shite does not constitute any form of commitment.

You can shite only once a day without having your manhood questioned.

The only apology you have to make after having a shite is if there are skid marks around the bowl.

Even a messy shite can be immensely satisfying.

You can read a book while having a shite without incurring your partner's wrath.

Women don't expect you to shite three times a night.

Your partner won't get jealous just because you've had a shite without telling her.

Your ultimate fantasy shite is absolutely free.

Nobody complains if you shite within ten seconds of sitting down.

A shite can be erased from the memory with a single flush.

'Bowling helps to take my mind off shite . . .'

You don't pay for a shite nine months later.

Her father doesn't come looking for you after a shite . . . unless you've broken the bowl.

In view of the evidence, therefore, it is no surprise that the dump scene is tipped to replace the sex scene as the 'must-have' ingredient in modern movies. Soon, actors willing to open their bowels on screen will be in greater demand than those who open their legs. The only difference is that the Hollywood casting couch will need plastic covers. And, in truth, Meg Ryan could have achieved the same degree of ecstasy – and made even louder noises – if she had simply done number twos in that restaurant. Here are a handful of cinema's greatest dumps:

In *The Life and Death of Peter Sellers*, Geoffrey Rush as Sellers is sitting on the toilet when Britt Ekland (Charlize Theron) walks in and announces that she is pregnant. An audible plop follows.

As Sydney Fuller in *D.O.A.*, Meg Ryan squats behind a dumpster in an alley. Movie buffs point out that it is definitely a number two since she discards her panties afterwards.

Ben Stiller is having a crap in Jennifer Aniston's apartment in *Along Came Polly* when he is interrupted by her pet ferret. Having run out of toilet paper, he instead uses a piece of sentimental embroidery that causes the toilet to overflow.

In *Demolition Man*, Sylvester Stallone plays a cop who is cryogenically frozen then thawed out in the future to track down his nemesis. He goes for a dump, only to find that they don't use toilet paper in the future.

Jane Fonda drops her load in *Fun With Dick and Jane* after carrying out her first robbery.

Robin Williams is pictured sitting in a low-sided cubicle in *Good Morning, Vietnam* while engaged in conversation with a fellow soldier.

In *Two Weeks Notice*, Sandra Bullock gets a sudden attack of the cramps while stuck in a traffic jam. She rushes to a nearby house where she drops explosive diarrhoea, the sound effects of which frighten the children. For the rest of the day she walks around with a telltale stain on her butt.

Dustin Hoffman is interrupted mid-dump by Robert DeNiro in *Meet the Fockers*. After finishing his shower, DeNiro parts the curtains to see Hoffman sitting on the loo, his pants around his ankles and a big grin on his face. DeNiro asks for privacy but Hoffman replies, 'I'm almost through.'

'Okay, dump scene, Take Fourteen, and . . . ACTION!'

Tom Hanks is seen squatting in bushes on a tropical island in *Castaway*.

In *Guarding Tess*, Nicolas Cage is interrupted in mid-dump by the ringing of his mobile. Hearing the President's voice on the phone, he automatically stands up out of respect.

And here are some movie sequels just waiting to happen:

> *Bridget Jones's Diarrhoea*
>
> *Lock, Stock and Two Smoking Bowels*
>
> *Easy Slider*
>
> *Trainsquatting*
>
> *The Stench Connection*
>
> *Forrest Dump*
>
> *Lady and the Cramp*
>
> *Wiping Miss Daisy*
>
> *Fecal Attraction*
>
> *The Man With the Golden Dung*

poop scoops

A man was covered in human excrement in 2001 when vandals pushed over the portable toilet he was using. To add insult to injury, Edmund Ware had to be rescued after the toilet door was wedged against the ground. The embarrassed thirty-five-year-old crawled out to find that crowds attending Ipswich Music Day had gathered round the cubicle to watch his plight. 'After I closed the door, I heard kids' voices outside,' he said. 'They kicked the toilet with me inside. It chucked out everything: the whole contents of the bathroom. There was blue chemicals and waste all over me.' Volunteers from the St John Ambulance gave him a lift home and strongly advised him to have a bath.

In an attempt to reduce the number of train crashes caused by deer wandering on to the tracks, officials in western Japan came up with the idea of scaring the deer off by coating the most affected areas of track with lion dung. The ploy certainly worked. From over two hundred deer-related accidents in 2002, there were none in the following twelve months.

The town of Pemberville, Ohio, staged a fascinating contest in 2004 whereby contestants had to pick items of food out of toilet bowls with their mouths. A fourteen-year-old girl proudly recounted how she shoved her head into a toilet bowl full of chicken gizzards, chicken necks, water, Worcester sauce and corn, and used her teeth to retrieve sixteen pieces of meat in the allotted time. It can surely be only a matter of time before the sport receives Olympic recognition.

When Valerie Goold goes on vacation, the only memento she brings home of her travels is the local brand of toilet paper. The San Diego schoolteacher has been collecting foreign toilet paper since 1983 and has around fifty different samples. She has a three-ply from Peru that has two white sheets and one pink, one from Germany with vertical stripes, and a commemorative one from a Zurich train depicting a couple dancing. 'And there's one from Warsaw that is the roughest stuff in the world,' she says. 'It feels like tree bark. Those Polish people must be really tough to be able to use that.'

poop scoops

Australian betting shop robber Jacob Smith was sentenced to ten years' imprisonment in 2002, after a lump of dog poo on his shoe helped identify him. He took the precaution of masking his face during the robbery but failed to notice that he had previously stepped in something unpleasant, which proceeded to leave a telltale print at the scene of the crime. By analysing the footprint, police were able to trace it to Smith. And, in a deed above and beyond the call of duty, they confirmed that it was his shoe by conducting a smell test. Perhaps it was the sniffer dog's day off.

A child, delivered by a woman in the washroom of a moving train in India, slipped down the toilet hole and was later found alive on the tracks.

Woken by the sound of splashing water, a Texan family found a baby opossum in the toilet of their mobile home. Robert Hamblen said he used a toilet brush to coax the animal from the bowl into a box, before releasing it outdoors.

Motorists in New Zealand were showered with sewage in 2002 after a septic tank truck exploded. The force of the blast blew out a window of a nearby hotel and sent debris flying into parked cars. Police closed the road in Dunedin for three hours while firefighters washed away a fifty-metre trail of sewage.

A Pennsylvania woman had to clean fragments of hundred dollar bills after discovering them in her dog's poop. Having found the pieces when she was clearing up her Doberman Pinscher Mia's mess, Sue Gadaleta had to wait patiently for another twenty-four hours for the remaining pieces to pass through the dog's body. Then she washed and assembled the fragments and took them to the bank where she was given new notes in place of the dirty money. The dog had apparently snatched two bills while Ms Gadaleta had been writing a cheque.

At first it was a giant column that soon took the shape of a supramundane mushroom.

US JOURNALIST
WILLIAM L. LAWRENCE

the smallest room

No matter how keenly anticipated the shite, the experience will feel hollow unless the setting is right. In the words of Kirstie Allsopp, it is a question of location, location, location. After all, how can you appreciate the finer points of the moment while surrounded by walls covered in graffiti, offering dubious sexual services? Public conveniences can be so frustrating, not least because the shiny toilet paper makes it difficult to write down the numbers. Shiny toilet paper, like war, what is it good for? Absolutely nothing. Certainly not for wiping your bottom. You end up with more mess than you started with, just spread over a different area. You might as well use rubber gloves or an aubergine.

Apart from the quality of the paper, the other thing we most readily complain about in the toilet is the temperature of the seat. Although a cold seat can send a shiver through the entire body, delaying the act of defecation until the muscles relax again, a warm seat is not necessarily a good omen either. When forced to use a public convenience, I personally prefer to think of the seat as virgin territory rather than be reminded by the heat emanating from it that it was home to the buttocks of a sweaty businessman just a couple of minutes earlier.

In the right hands, toilet seats can be veritable *objets d'art*.

Barney Smith runs his own museum in Texas, boasting over seven hundred different styles of toilet seat. He was first inspired by fitting a set of deer antlers to a toilet seat as a wall mounting, although thankfully he has chosen not to replicate that particular design in areas intended for actual seating. However, his colourful designs pale in comparison to the $105,000

'Somewhere out there my father's remains are stuck to a Texas toilet seat.'

gem-studded toilet seat that Hollywood actor Ben Affleck bought for fiancée Jennifer Lopez in 2003. The seat was encrusted with rubies, sapphires, pearls and a diamond, all of which were set in plastic so that J-Lo's prize asset would not get scratched. Despite – or maybe because of – this token of love, the couple broke up shortly afterwards. Diamonds may be a girl's best friend, but not when she's sitting on them.

Of course, in many parts of the world the toilet seat is an alien concept. In Turkey, Asia, the Middle East, and rural regions of France, Italy, Greece, and Portugal, the squat toilet prevails. In Turkey the user puts his or her feet on footrests and faces the entrance to the cubicle before squatting down to defecate. In Japan, however, the user faces the toilet. British tourists often refer to these devices as 'stand and deliver' toilets. Advocates of squatters' rights point out that the position of the body helps relieve constipation and other disorders and that, because there is no contact between bare skin and a potentially dirty surface, the risk of contamination is also reduced. Moreover, squat toilets are cheaper to clean, less vulnerable to vandalism than sitting toilets, and they encourage rapid turnover since there is little point in taking any reading matter unless you are a fully qualified contortionist. And herein lies the problem that I have with squat toilets. Quite apart from the fact that they are dangerous and slippery, that bad aim can leave the surrounding floor badly soiled, and that, in places such as Greece and Turkey where the toilets do not have a flushing mechanism, it is all too easy for the inexperienced user to clog the toilet with paper, my principal objection to them is that they deny the user the full pleasures of a dump. In this hectic world, the toilet is an oasis of calm, a haven of peace away from the hustle and bustle of everyday life, a place where, for a few minutes each day, we can enter a fantasy world of love and beauty, culminating in a loud plop and the kind of stench usually reserved for when the Grand National field raise their tails in unison. But without the opportunity to read a magazine, do the crossword or sit quietly contemplating the meaning of life, the overall experience is devalued.

Fortunately, some people still know how to make a visit to the toilet a moment to treasure. In Hong Kong, jeweller Lam Sai-wing has built the world's most expensive washroom – a $4.8 million palace boasting two toilets made of 24-carat gold and encrusted with gems. The ceiling is decorated with 6,200 precious stones and the floor is embedded with gold bars. The only drawback is that customers, who must remove their shoes to avoid scratching the gold tiles, have to buy a minimum $200 worth of Lam's jewellery before using his facilities. The phrase 'spending a penny' has clearly fallen victim to gross inflation.

Splendid though such opulence may be, for traditionalists nothing will ever replace the outside loo. Of all the things that have vanished from society over the past forty years – the bobby on the beat, discipline in schools, *Noel's House Party* – none has been so greatly mourned as the outside loo. Nothing could match the sheer delight of sitting at the end of the garden, gazing up at the stars, knowing that you were in total privacy apart from the dozen spiders and occasional woodland creature scurrying around your ankles. A trawl of the byways of Britain will still unearth a few of these blasts from the past but generally they have disappeared under a swathe of decking. Surprisingly. for a nation that gave us McDonald's and Dan Quayle, the United States does possess some style, and devotees continue to worship the Great American Outhouse. Families decorate them at Christmas, a man in New Hampshire recently sold his for $800, and each year the town of Trenary, Michigan, hosts the Trenary Outhouse Classic where teams of two push specially built outhouses on skis down a 500-foot (150m) racecourse. It is sport at its very best, and an event to which *Grandstand* will no doubt soon be devoting an entire Saturday afternoon.

'You can never find a toilet on skis when you really need one . . .'

THE WORLD OF SHITE

Away from the serious business of studying faeces, there is
nothing I enjoy more than testing my fellow professionals on
place names with scatological connotations. For example, did
you know there are two Shits in Iran, although obviously the
number will rise to three if Bush invades? Here are some more
from around the world:

Anus	Indonesia
Ars	Iran
Bottom	North Carolina
Bum	Azerbaijan
Bumbang	Australia
Crap	Albania
Dikshit	India
Dump	Jamaica
Lake do Dungo	Angola
Poo	Spain
Lake de Poopo	Bolivia
Shit	Ethiopia
Turdo	Romania

TEN CHOICE EUPHEMISMS FOR TAKING A DUMP

Releasing the chocolate hostage

Sending some sailors to sea

Dropping a wad in the porcelain god

Firing rear thrusters

Letting a brown snake out of the cave

Dropping one from the poopdeck

Doing business with John

Making a deposit in the porcelain bank

Dropping some friends off at the pool

William Shatnering

There are passages of Ulysses which can be read only in the toilet – if one wants to extract the full flavour of their content.

HENRY MILLER, *BLACK SPRING*

what's dung
is dung

In this age of recycling, nothing could be more natural than putting human waste to practical use. Ever since Stone Age Man realised that woolly mammoth manure was more beneficial to his roses than in a broth, society has been quick to spot the potential of dung – as a fuel, in medicine, as a building material, as a love potion, and even as a fashion accessory.

It has been estimated that within the next hundred years, the world's supply of fuels such as oil and gas will disappear altogether. Scientists have spent decades trying to invent fresh ways of harnessing energy from the sun or the wind, but recently, boffins in Thailand have come up with an ingenious solution. They have been retrieving excrement from prisoners and recycling it into fuel to be used in cars. If sufficient

'As a qualified Diesel Fitter, I'd really rather not have to change my job title.'

automobile manufacturers can be persuaded to adapt their engines, dung could be the new diesel.

Only last year, the Science Museum in London announced that it was planning to reduce its energy bills by using human excrement. The idea is to siphon the waste from the museum's fourteen toilet blocks, store it and then either burn it as fuel in a mini-power station or turn it into electricity using a microbial fuel cell. The museum calculated that the excrement from its three million visitors each year would generate enough power for fifteen thousand lightbulbs. 'It would be a great way for visitors to give something back to the museum,' said a spokesman.

Animal faeces are equally in demand as a source of power. In India, towering piles of cow dung are dried and used as fuel for cooking and heating, while Australian farmers are gathering pig poop to generate electricity. And Canada's Toronto Zoo is planning to use 1,900 tonnes of dung produced by the zoo animals to generate power for heating and lighting – one elephant with diarrhoea could probably keep the entire place going for a year.

Fresh cow manure is also used to build houses in India. It is made into a plaster-like paste, which is then applied to timber or stone walls. When dried, the manure is rock hard, providing the perfect organic home, albeit one that is somewhat susceptible to fire.

'What a charming scent your soap has, my dear. Pig shit, isn't it?'

And how many people know that some animal faeces boast medicinal or cleansing properties? Ass dung was once used to cure skin blemishes, hare excrement was said to cure sagging breasts, and camel dung used to be rubbed into the scalp to give hair a natural wave. To this day, a traditional cure for baldness in Norway is to smear the head with cow dung for twenty minutes twice a week. Cow dung serves a different purpose in parts of India where a coating is still seen as the best cure for people struck by lightning. In the early twentieth century, cakes of animal excrement, particularly pig manure, were employed as an alternative to soap in some areas of Britain. Apparently the women became so accustomed to the familiar stench on washdays that when soap was eventually introduced they often moaned that the suds made them feel sick. And recently an oil company in Dubai discovered that the plentiful supplies of local camel dung proved effective in cleaning up soil contaminated by oil and chemical spillage.

During the Middle Ages, women concocted an illegal potion made of their own excrement that was intended to make them irresistible to the opposite sex. The idea that a man could fall hopelessly in love with a woman by eating her faeces may sound far-fetched, but women will point out that they have been swallowing crap from men for years. Anyway, the authorities took the aphrodisiac powers of dung

'Once you've tasted my shit, I'm irresistible.'

seriously enough to rule that anybody found brewing the love potion should be put to death.

A sobering thought the next time you visit Starbucks is that the world's most expensive coffee is made from animal excrement. The rare delicacy Kopi Luwak sells for $300 per pound and is made from beans that have been eaten by and passed through the digestive tract of the common palm civet, a native of Indonesia.

Picnics in eighteenth century Britain could be a pungent affair because the gentry liked to garnish their mustard and cress salads with horse dung while cheese lovers might like to know that a recommended recipe for the Indian cheese *paneer* is to smoke it in dung and eat it with pasta.

Nor must we overlook the value of poop in fashion. At one of Alaska's liveliest events, the Annual Moose Dropping Festival at Talkeetna, visitors can purchase earrings and necklaces made from moose droppings coated in varnish. Another highlight of the festival is a moose-dropping throwing competition, where a dried pat or 'chip' is hurled as far as possible. So remember not to ask for chips with your meal in Alaska.

Men are always wicked at bottom unless they are made good by some compulsion.

NICCOLO MACHIAVELLI

poop scoops

Moulay Ismael, a Sultan of Morocco in the seventeenth century, presented samples of his bowel movements to the ladies of the court as a sign of affection.

Remote tribes in Borneo and Brazil believe that human excrement has mystical powers and insist on burying it to ward off evil spirits.

According to most sources, the longest ever turd was produced by an American gentleman who managed a mighty 12ft 2in (3.7m) brown python over a period of 2hr 12min. What is generally believed to be the world's widest turd was excreted by a twenty-one-stone man and measured four inches (10 cm) in width for most of its eight-inch (20 cm) length. As these sightings have never been verified, however, they may be like the fisherman's tale of 'the one that got away'.

Germanic tribes of the third century used to hide their valuables in pits beneath layers of excrement to prevent thieves from searching for them.

Forty-nine per cent of men and 26 per cent of women read in the toilet.

The Romanian economy was in such dire straits in the 1990s that toilet paper was made from shredded bank notes.

At the court of Louis XIV, nobles actually paid for the honour of watching the king defecating last thing at night before bed.

Britain's 6.2 million dogs produce 900 tons of waste a day.

**O that the spirit
could remain
tinged but untarnished
by its strain!**

US POET ROBERT LOWELL 'WAKING
EARLY ONE SUNDAY MORNING.'

wild about
shite

When asked which living creature they would choose to be, most humans opt for something like the lion, the golden eagle or the great white shark. But for me, there is only one contender: the dung beetle. For this little chap can push dung four times its own size – a sensation that many of us can identify with after a bout of constipation. Its diet consists almost entirely of dung, which provides all the nutrients it requires. Indeed, it doesn't even need to drink water. The female lays its eggs in a dung ball and can actually find excrement before the animal has finished producing it – a gift for which I would swap my fifty metres breaststroke certificate any day. The dung beetle may be the star of the show, but many more members of the natural world have fascinating attachments to their faeces.

Beaver poo often floats because it contains so much undigested wood.

An elephant produces fifty pounds (22.7 kg) of dung every day — enough to fill the trunk of a family car.

Sea cucumbers are detritus feeders, so their poo consists mainly of sand. It comes in the form of a pretty, white, coiled rosette that people often pick up, unaware of what it is.

Rabbits produce five hundred pellets of poo every day. They often deposit their droppings in heaps to mark territory.

Fox poo comes in different colours. Those that live in urban areas and eat human leftovers produce brown stools, but those that live in the countryside and eat mice and rabbits produce white stools, on account of the phosphate in the bones that they have digested. So, if you want your dog to produce white stools, give him plenty of bones.

Llama dung is relatively odourless.

Mole rats have special toilet chambers in their underground burrows where they enjoy rolling in their own excrement.

If food is hard to find, young cockroaches survive by eating their parents' faeces.

Cows poo on average sixteen times a day.

Mice feeding on coloured crayons will produce droppings based on the colour of the crayon they were nibbling.

The skipper caterpillar is just an inch-and-a-half (3.8 cm) long but it can shoot crap a distance of six feet (1.83 m).

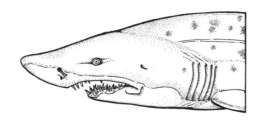

Sharks can detect the smell of their prey's faeces from over a mile away.

Deer droppings are called fewmets. They are cylindrical in shape, usually with one pointed end.

Otter droppings are called spraints. They are black and sticky when fresh and smell slightly fishy.

Termite colonies use their own poo to help build castles as tall as a house.

On average, geese poo once every twelve minutes.

Sloths only poo once a week.

If your loft is infested with rats, pray for brown rats because they are much tidier. They place their faeces in corners or along walls, whereas black rats spread theirs over the whole floor without any consideration for others.

Fox droppings are twisted with long tapering ends.

Badgers dig special latrines in the ground and may poo in the same hole several times.

Over a period of six months, a pair of mice will produce eighteen thousand droppings.

Llamas use a communal dung pile.

The Egyptian vulture eats its own poo to make itself more attractive to the opposite sex.

In addition to familiar dry droppings, rabbits produce soft, slimy poo, which they eat as soon as it is produced. They swallow the soft poo whole, without chewing it, and recycle it in order to derive maximum benefit from the food. When they drop it for the second time, it comes out in the form of the hard, dry pellet.

And meanwhile time goes about its immemorial work of making everyone look and feel like shit.

MARTIN AMIS, *LONDON FIELDS*

hot on the
market

Have you always dreamed of being able to send your loved one a heart-shaped turd? Or perhaps a poo in the shape of a cuddly teddy bear? Well, now those dreams can come true thanks to the Turd Twister, an ingenious American device that shapes your turd into different designs. For just $9.95, it fits comfortably up your backside and, according to the shape you select,

'Here's some I made earlier.'

will produce logs in a myriad of different designs, including a four-leafed clover, a Christmas tree, a star, skull and crossbones, a flying bat and many more. 'Simply insert the apparatus. Take a dump, and watch the results!' say the manufacturers. 'Fun for the whole family!' Even if you're a fan of gag gifts, this will make you gag.

United States toy manufacturers have introduced a new range called Poop Pals. Squeeze the tummy of these cute, furry pets and a jelly bean pops out of their bum.

'Did I really spend all those years at college just to end up inventing new flavours of jelly bean for some kid to shoot out of a cuddly toy's arse?'

At $5 a time, a US company offers the DooDoo Doodler, a poop-shaped pen described as ideal for writing to your ex-spouse. Advantages over traditional writing implements are that nobody ever steals it and it will almost certainly cure you of that nasty pen chewing habit.

Joanna Gair, an expatriate Scottish woman living in Tasmania, is turning kangaroo and wallaby droppings into money by transforming them into writing paper. The droppings are boiled for five hours before being pulped and rinsed with water. The natural fibre left behind is then mixed with recycled paper and turned into sand-coloured writing paper, greetings cards and envelopes. She relies heavily on public donations of marsupial dung to make the paper, which is marketed as Roo Poo.

Monthly Doos is a calendar devoted to the virtues of dog poo. Each month features a different scene, photographed by professionals, but enhanced – both digitally and spiritually – by the addition of a pile of steaming dog mess. The pictures are so realistic they almost take your breath away.

Marketed in the US, the Brief Safe is the ultimate in crime prevention. It consists of a pair of underpants with a giant brown skid mark on the back and a secret Velcro-fastening pocket at the front. Manufacturers Shomer-Tec say that if you hide your valuables in the secret pouch and then drape the pants over a wash basket or in a suitcase so that the skid mark is clearly visible, no self-respecting burglar will go near them.

poop scoops

When he lost his high-powered computer-programming job in 2002, Steve Relles didn't sit on his backside. Instead he went into business scooping up dog droppings around his home in Delmar, New York State. The 'Delmar Dog Butler', as he calls himself, already has over one hundred clients who pay $10 each for a once-a-week cleaning of their yard. 'I can clean four to five yards in an hour if they are close together,' says the forty-two-year-old entrepreneur. 'St Bernards are my favourite customers since they poop in large piles which are easy to find.'

In 2004, inventor Leonard van Munster unveiled an Amsterdam toilet that commented on users' actions. Fitted with sensors to detect the visitors' motions, the talking toilet could remind you to wash your hands, lift the seat or point out the previous user failed to obey the rules of hygiene.

Two Germans searching for a toilet at Frankfurt Airport in 2000 took a wrong turning and ended up on a plane to Moscow.

A Cambridgeshire village has erected a 5ft-tall statue of dinosaur poo to celebrate its past. Bassingbourn parish council chose the sculpture because the region profited from the discovery of fossilized dinosaur droppings in the late nineteenth century.

A forty-year-old Florida woman was so fat she was unable to move from her couch for six years. When emergency workers discovered her in 2004, they had to wear protective gear since in that period she had never managed to get up and go to the bathroom. Firefighters struggled in vain to free her, and she later died in hospital, still attached to the couch.

A California woman was sentenced to 120 hours' community service in 2005, after placing dog poo in her stepson's schoolbag. Deborah Machnick took the tough stance to punish the boy when he failed to clear up after his pet. He has since left home and joined the military.

poop scoops

Taught by his hiking club never to leave garbage behind, a youth in Israel set fire to used toilet paper after relieving himself. But the fire destroyed 667 acres of scrubland and took all night to bring under control. Hundreds of tourists were evacuated from the area.

A sixty-five-year-old guest at a Milan hotel slipped as he stepped out of the shower in 2002, accidentally jamming his hand down the funnel of the toilet while trying to break his fall. He was stuck there for an hour before being rescued.

A restaurant in Kaohsiung, Taiwan, has cleaned up by serving food on toilet-shaped plates. The toilet-themed eaterie, where diners sit on toilet seats beneath lamps converted from urinals, is the brainchild of owner Eric Wang who first made his fortune by selling ice cream in toilet-shaped cones. The idea for that came from a popular Japanese comic which featured a robot doll fond of eating excrement in ice cream cones.

A Chicago thief who tried to steal an expensive diamond in 2003 by swallowing it and replacing it with a fake was arrested when staff at the jeweller's spotted the switch. Police sifted through his bowel movements for five days until the incriminating gem finally emerged.

UK toilet manufacturers Twyfords are reported to be designing a 'smart toilet' that can automatically conduct urine and fecal analysis for users and then send the results to the family doctor via the Internet in the event of the readings being abnormal.

A rebellious US prisoner recently paid the ultimate price for his lack of hygiene. After defecating on the floor of his cell, he slipped in his own faeces, struck his head on the ground and was killed.

A total of 273 envelopes containing human excrement were recently sent anonymously to every member of South Korea's National Assembly. It was thought the special delivery constituted some sort of protest.

What does not destroy me, makes me strong.
FRIEDRICH NIETZSCHE

ask
Dr Julian:

your questions answered

Dear Dr Julian,
What kind of diet should I follow if I want to produce massive
quantities of the brown stuff?

Eat plenty of fibre – lots of fruit and vegetables – for soft poos.
If you want to produce hard turds, reduce your fibre and eat
binding foods that are high in protein. People on the Atkins diet
are renowned for their hard stools. The GI diet may prove a
better bet – but you shouldn't eat a whole platoon.

Dear Dr Julian,
Why is it that no matter how thoroughly I chew sweetcorn, it always
appears in my stools as whole kernels?

This is probably the question I am asked more than any other
and the corn poop phenomenon does indeed appear to be one
of life's great mysteries. What actually happens is that when we
chew corn, the yellow outer coating comes away from the inner
kernel. The coating is composed almost entirely of cellulose
and, as such, is indigestible. Consequently, it passes through the
digestive tract untouched and emerges in our stools looking to

all the world like a whole kernel when in fact it is mainly just the outer skin. By contrast, the inside of the corn is soft, starchy and easy to digest, and that is the part that we manage to chew. So the whole process is like a digestive magic trick, an intestinal illusion.

Dear Dr Julian,
Why aren't there more television programmes dedicated to defecation?

Watch out for the new ITV Saturday evening series *Stars in Their Stools* where celebrities masquerade as turds and vice-versa. Then there's *Celebrity Big Job* on Channel 4, where viewers vote for an E-list celebrity to be evacuated from the house each week, and the return of the popular talent show *New Faeces*. In the meantime there's always the long-running *Loose Women*.

Dear Dr Julian,
What sort of turd will I produce after taking cocaine?

We call it Charlie Brown.

Dear Dr Julian,
I have always wanted to produce a nice stool with red stripes in it but I don't want to bleed for my art. Any suggestions?

Try eating pimentos. Like sweetcorn, some other brightly-coloured foods pass through the gut almost unchanged, so pimentos should give you some striking red blotches in your stools. My aunt Ada swears by them and has had several of her gaily-coloured turds exhibited in her local village hall.

Dear Dr Julian,
I read recently in our parish magazine that some couples become sexually aroused by faeces. Can this be true or was the vicar making it up?

Yes, some people do derive sexual excitement from faeces. The practice is known as coprophilia and brings a whole new meaning to the phrase 'hot and steamy'. The habit of defecating on a person to derive sexual pleasure is commonly called 'brown showers', but it is not to be recommended, especially if you have a white carpet. It takes ages to get the stains off . . . so I'm told.

Dear Dr Julian,
Why is bird poo white?

Unlike mammals, birds don't urinate. It's all or nothing with birds: no half measures. What happens is that their kidneys extract nitrogenous wastes from the bloodstream, but instead of excreting it as urea dissolved in urine as humans do, they excrete it in the form of uric acid. And because uric acid has a very low solubility in water, it emerges as a white paste, the principal property of which appears to be that it has a particular attraction to newly-washed cars.

Dear Dr Julian,
Have you ever left the toilet seat up after use?

Many of us have had wild student days where we've done things we'd rather forget. Some took drugs, others drank themselves into oblivion, but yes, I confess, there were times – maybe only once or twice – when I did forget to put the toilet seat down after use.

Dear Dr Julian,
Why does some poo float?

Floaters are turds that have an unusually high gas content. For the most part, the gases produced by bacteria in our gut merge into a large fart bubble, which can have devastating consequences for anyone not suffering from a serious head cold. However, these gases sometimes remain dispersed in the faeces instead. The resultant poop comes out foamy and has a lower density than water, therefore it rises to the surface. Poo with a high fat content also floats.

Dear Dr Julian,
Do you ever wipe more than once with the same piece of toilet paper?

Certainly. Toilet paper is an expensive commodity so it doesn't pay to be wasteful. If a sheet is only slightly soiled, I see no reason not to fold it over and re-use it for the next wipe. Incidentally, this practice is known in the trade as double dipping.

Dear Dr Julian,
Why is it that sometimes my poo comes out in a long chain but on other occasions it breaks into pieces?

I'm glad you asked me that. You see, if left to its own devices, your poo would emerge in a soft unbroken length, in much the same way that sausage meat comes out of a machine. But with the exertion of pushing out, your anal sphincter contracts and pinches off lengths of the poo as it emerges. If you pinch hard enough, the poo breaks into pieces; if you only pinch slightly, it might stay linked together, like a string of sausages. And, of course, if you remain totally relaxed and refrain from contracting, you can produce a poo of epic proportions that will be the envy of your friends.

Dear Dr Julian,
What is the truth about blue ice? Does it exist or is it just a pigment of my imagination?

Ah, old blue ice is back. That perennial question. Well, it's certainly not a myth and is all too real for people who live under airline flight paths. Airlines are not permitted to dump lavatory waste while in flight but leaks do occur in the toilets. In such instances, the mixture of human waste and liquid disinfectant freezes at very high altitudes and forms ice on the aircraft. As the plane descends, the ice warms and falls to the ground, often on unsuspecting houses. It takes its blue hue from the disinfectant, although victims have also reported being bombarded with purple, black or grey ice. In 2003, a man from California received over $3,000 in compensation after two chunks of blue ice smashed through the skylight of his boat. At lower altitudes, blue ice falls in liquid form, which causes less damage but is considerably less pleasant.

Dear Dr Julian,
Is it true that eating meat makes your poo smell worse?

Well, meat protein is rich in sulphides, which result in exceptionally smelly farts and poo. But while many experts state that this gives them the edge over vegetarians' poos, have you ever tried standing outside the toilets at a vegans' convention for more than thirty seconds? Think of a cross between a baby's soiled nappy and the giraffe house at the zoo.

Kuso	Japan
Lanta	Finland
Majon	Spain
Merda	Italy
Merde	France
Mist	Germany
Seprõ	Hungary
Skata	Greece
Skeet	Denmark
Tahi	Malaysia
Tutti	Hindi
Uchra	Arabic

Noise proves nothing. Often a hen who has merely laid an egg cackles as if she had laid an asteroid.

MARK TWAIN

martyrs to their bowels

It is in the very nature of celebrity that we do not expect physical imperfection in our heroes. Would we have worshipped Debbie Harry if she had a glass eye, Tom Cruise if he had head lice or Lassie if she suffered from hard pad? It's the same with bowels. Somehow, we do not imagine the idols of stage and screen going to the toilet. How many photos do you see of Sophia Loren squatting on the bog, straining and grimacing, with her knickers around her ankles? Yet the fact is that celebrities are only human, although some disguise it better than others, and as such they suffer from the same afflictions as the man in the street. All manner of famous people have suffered hideously from piles – William Wordsworth, Charles Dickens and Anton Chekhov to name but three. Napoleon had such horrendous haemorrhoids at Waterloo that he was scarcely able to sit on his horse – a frailty that arguably contributed to his defeat. Even the legendary lover Casanova was stricken with piles. Given that he claimed to have bedded hundreds of women, how many more escaped his voracious clutches because he was applying ointment to the troubled area? Another with pile problems was *Carry On* star Kenneth Williams, a man who was generally obsessed with his bowels. He suffered terribly from haemorrhoids and consequently had a

'I say! Did you hear that poor old Dickens has got piles?'

deep-seated mistrust of other people's toilets. Whenever he moved into a theatre for a play, he always insisted on having his own personal toilet, for his sole use. Similarly, any visitors to his London flat were never permitted to use the toilet there – instead they had to go to nearby Tottenham Court Road tube station.

King Ferdinand IV of Naples, who ruled in the latter half of the eighteenth century, suffered from severe constipation. Each visit to the toilet was such an event that he liked to have an audience to keep him entertained while he strained. Among those privy to these unlikely gatherings was his father-in-law, the Austrian Emperor Joseph, who recalled watching proceedings for over half an hour, until the 'terrible stench' convinced all present that it was over. Apparently, Ferdinand also liked to show his father-in-law the end product for closer inspection.

'The King wants me to watch him do WHAT?'

Although Elvis was the most famous bathroom casualty, he was by no means alone. Catherine the Great of Russia suffered a massive stroke while sitting on the toilet and fell off, dead. For a woman renowned for her libido and toyboys, it was a particularly undignified way to go.

Hitler and Queen Victoria both suffered dreadfully from flatulence, as did Louis XIV. Nevertheless, the French monarch was rather proud of his wind and demonstrated his admiration for his sister-in-law, the Duchess of Orléans, by farting loudly in her presence. A newspaper of the time would surely have summed up his prowess with the headline: 'The Sun King Shines Out of His Arse.'

poop scoops

A concerned Canadian citizen dressed up as a 6ft (1.83m) turd in 2005 to protest against a city's dumping of raw sewage into the Pacific Ocean. In his role as the official voice of POOP (People Opposed to Outfall Pollution), James Skwarok, aka 'Mr Floatie', argued that the practice of flushing some thirty million gallons of sewage daily into the ocean was harmful. Barred from a political meeting at Victoria, British Columbia, apparently for looking too realistic, he had to settle for passing toilet paper business cards.

A South African woman won damages of $7,000 after a toilet collapsed beneath her. Susanna Jacoba de Beer was visiting her husband in a Pretoria military hospital in 1999 when she needed to visit the toilet. With the ladies' out of order, she was directed to the gents' but no sooner had she sat down than the toilet bowl shattered beneath her. The cistern also fell down, leaving her right leg trapped under rubble.

To cater for people who like to read on the toilet, German publisher Georges Hemmerstoffer announced a new range of novels and poems printed on toilet paper. 'It will save readers taking a newspaper into the bathroom,' he explained. 'We want our books to be used.'

A Norwegian woman got the shock of her life when she sat on the toilet at her home in Sandnes . . . and saw a rat pop its head out between her legs. A traumatized Marit Graeter jumped from the seat in horror, and the rodent disappeared back down the plumbing. She vowed never to use the downstairs toilet again.

Postal worker James M. Beal of Empire, Michigan, splattered porcupine faeces on his colleagues after being sacked for poor job performance. The day after his dismissal, he returned with two five-gallon buckets filled with faeces from the woods and hurled them over his workmates.

poop scoops

Michigan resident Bill Jarrett knows just about everything there is to know about toilet paper. He has been on a roll for three decades, collecting hundreds of documents relating to toilet paper and painstakingly analysing the toilet habits of the American public. He is particularly keen to resolve the great toilet paper debate – whether the roll should be placed in such a way that the paper hangs next to or away from the wall, or, as aficionados refer to it, under or over. The 'under' fraternity say that the overall artistic effect is more streamlined with the loose end tucked against the wall and that it is more difficult for dogs to unravel since errant puppies generally go for the roll itself rather than the hanging paper. Also, with the paper dangling in mid-air, tearing it off can be a two-handed job, thus increasing the risk of getting germs on the paper. However, the 'over' school counter that placing the paper next to the wall creates a hygiene problem since the user is more likely to touch the surface behind the roll with dirty hands. They also say that 'over' is the only way to hang patterned toilet paper, otherwise the pattern will show up backwards. In a recent poll by a US toilet paper manufacturer, 72 per cent of toilet users interviewed voted in favour of 'over', but Bill Jarrett wants a national referendum to determine a uniform way of hanging toilet paper and to put an end to an argument that has been raging for 150 years.

An off-duty policeman's gun went off twice as he pulled down his pants to use the toilet, injuring a bystander in the process. Officer Craig Clancy was attending a 2005 car auction in San Antonio, Texas, when nature called. As he undid his trousers, his gun fell from its holster but in trying to catch it he grabbed the trigger by mistake and fired two bullets. One bullet went through the wall of the cubicle and grazed the leg of a man who was washing his hands. The police department was said to be investigating the incident.

Study to be quiet, and to do your own business.

1 THESSALONIANS, 4:2

how do you shite?

Use this brief questionnaire to establish just how good your toilet etiquette really is.

1. You go into the bathroom to be confronted by a dreadful stench. Do you

a) Spray some air freshener

b) Hold your nose and press on regardless

c) Shout out 'Who the hell's dropped a stinkbomb?'

2. You're part-way through wiping when you run out of toilet paper. Do you

a) Shuffle downstairs with your pants around your ankles

b) Call for someone to bring you a roll

c) Wipe your arse on the towel and hope nobody will notice

3. As you flush, you see you have left skid marks around the bowl. Do you

a) Shrug your shoulders and leave

b) Pour in some toilet cleaner

c) Remove the stains by pissing on them

4. You have dropped a really impressive log. Do you

a) Quietly congratulate yourself before flushing it away

b) Call out, 'Hey, everyone, take a look at this beauty!'

c) Search for a tape measure

5. Your wife nags you for failing to put the seat down. Do you

    a) Promise to try and remember in future

    b) Point out all her annoying habits

    c) Bury the body under the patio

6. You're alone in the house and mid-shite when the doorbell rings. Do you

    a) Ignore it and hope that the caller will go away

    b) Yell out, 'I won't be a moment'

    c) Ram a wad of toilet paper up your backside and waddle downstairs

7. A particularly long and recalcitrant turd refuses to flush away. Do you

   a) Hope that the next user will deal with it

   b) Try and get rid of it yourself

   c) Hold your wife's ankles while she goes in after it

Scores:
1. a) 5 b) 3 c) 1   **2.** a) 3 b) 5 c) 1   **3.** a) 1 b) 5 c) 3

4. a) 5 b) 3 c) 1   **5.** a) 5 b) 3 c) 1   **6.** a) 3 b) 5 c) 1

7. a) 1 b) 5 c) 3

How you rate: 7-13 Your bathroom habits leave a lot to be desired. 14-24 Room for improvement. 25-35 You are properly toilet trained.

now wash
your hands